DO YOU SCRATCH YOUR BOTTOM IN THE BATH?

Have it reglazed by the professional

DO YOU SCRATCH YOUR BOTTOM IN THE BATH?
Have it reglazed by the professional

A Collection of Public Notices, Advertisements,
Announcements, Instructions, Warnings, Exhortations,
and Gobbledegook

selected and introduced by
Michael R. Turner

Illustrated by Gof

SOUVENIR PRESS

First published 1998 by
Souvenir Press Ltd,
43 Great Russell Street, London WC1B 3PA

ISBN 0 285 63464 X

Typeset by Rowland Phototypesetting Ltd,
Bury St Edmunds, Suffolk

Printed in Great Britain by
The Bath Press Ltd, Bath

Contents

PREFACE

We are bombarded by public notices. From all sides they come—government departments, advertisers large and small, manufacturers, churches, local authorities, local shops and restaurants: anyone with a message for our eyes and ears. We meet them on road signs, posters, leaflets, official forms, statements by spokespersons, even on cards in newsagents' windows.

Most of these communications are eminently forgettable. A precious minority, however, are different, for the messages they carry to the public are not exactly what their authors intended. They are unintentionally hilarious: literary banana skins.

Spare a thought for the mostly anonymous authors of these gems. They live unrecognised and they seldom if ever realise the full impact of their labours. Without their well-meaning but flawed endeavours life would be much duller than it is.

This selection constitutes a modest archive of the present state of public communication. Other collectors have already worked assiduously in the field to record the wonder and variety of the genre. The tailpieces to the *Daily Telegraph*'s 'Peterborough' column, *Private Eye*'s boobs and misprints and *The Times* letters pages have been rich secondary sources for this anthology, as have such wide-ranging compilations as John G. (Jock)

Murray's enchanting *A Gentleman Publisher's Commonplace Book* and, in the United States, Willard R. Espy's two Almanacks of *Words at Play*. As for primary sources, *The Times* Personal Column and small advertisements in a variety of newspapers and magazines are mines of bizarre items. The World-Wide Web has yet to fulfil its obvious promise, but a first cuckoo of what will undoubtedly be a fecund spring is in captivity here.

Thanks are due to Olaf Sargint, Joan Bailey, Guy Penman, John Coldstream and many others who have found for me some of the most glittering jewels. Above all, I am grateful to all those who, albeit unwittingly, have written this book.

MRT

TELL THE WORLD

Addressing the multitude seems to produce a strange loss of self-control in both the professional copywriter and the humble composer of a card for the newsagent's window. Pride in the product replaces the rules of grammar, syntax and decorum, with happy results.

Sign outside a Sussex farm
Horse manure bagged 75p. Do it yourself 10p.

Large hoarding in New Delhi
GREAT COSMIC UNIVERSAL STORES
Also behind Railway Station

Shop advertisement
Exclusive universal tailors

Notice in a West Country shop
Bric-a-brac bought
Antiques sold

Advertisement in the Washington Star
The reason why we can sell our antiques for less is because we buy them direct from the manufacturer

*Notice in a jeweller's window in Cork, spotted
by Dervla Murphy*

Ears pierced while you wait.

Leaflet distributed through London letter-boxes

Thames Water customers can now get cheaper gas
from London Electricity.

And in the Western Gazette, *announcing a new
members' meeting of the Blandford Young
Farmers Club*

WAKE UP WITH A YOUNG FARMER!

From the price list of a San Francisco novelty store

Bring your kids up to date. Superb color-printed
Globe of the World. Can be blown up in
seconds.

Notice in a Berkshire village hall

Coming events. Tuesday, July 22.
No WI whist drive.

And one outside a West Midlands public house

Good Clean Entertainment Every Night
Except Thursday

Card in a jeweller's window

Genuine simulated pearls

Advertisement in the South Wales Echo
D. CAESAR JONES
FUNERAL DIRECTORS
Christmas Parties, Christmas Day Lunch
PANTBACH ROAD, RHIWBINA
Private Chapel of Rest

Leaflet distributed in Walton-on-Thames
As your newsagent, we are pleased to announce we
can now offer you a fully comprehensive shoe
repair service.

Advertisement in What's On in London
First time ever in Britain: NUDES on REAL ICE

And in the Gainsborough News
Hundreds of satisfied women can't be wrong: take a
trip down to Fred's.

Entry in a publisher's stock list
The Way to Camp (*limp*)

London shop sign
Same day cleaners. 48 hours service

Boast by an Indianapolis undertaker
Our caskets all come with a lifetime guarantee.

. . . The deceased was allergic to flowers.

From the Newbury Weekly News

JUNE 23   THE WINTER'S TALE
& The Festival of Sheepshearing
in the gardens beside the river
by W. Shakespeare
Sponsored by Rank Xerox plc

And from The Sunday Times

If he gets through the day on pills, see that he
does it beautifully. Give him a crocodile-skin
pill box.

While this advertisement for The Listener, *published in*
Radio Times, *claimed:*

The book reviews are so good and informative, you
feel you don't need to read the books.

Sign on a market stall in Yorkshire

Nightdresses slashed in half!

An advertisement in the Sydney Morning Herald

NOMADIC RUG TRADERS
Specialists in old Oriental Rugs and Kilims
HAVE MOVED

Obituary notice in a New York newspaper

Members of the family request mourners to omit floral
tributes. The deceased was allergic to flowers.

Instruction on a leaflet with a pack of contraceptives
Don't return used condoms to the distributor
through the mail.

Notice in a draper's shop
If it's quality you want, try us. The best is none
too good.

And one in the Windsor Express
Hundreds use our service. They know no
better.

Advertisement in a local Irish newspaper
Deno's—stocks practically all leading brands
of liquor. Funerals undertaken at short notice.

Seen in a souvenir shop in Amman
Our boast—we never allow a dissatisfied customer to
leave this store.

*Elegantly executed sign at the Lost Gardens of Heligan,
Cornwall*
LADIES
DISABLED
and
BABY
CHANGING

Also from Cornwall, a sign on scaffolding in a narrow village street

Sorry
Builders

Announcement in a country newspaper

Notice is hereby given that after this date the owners of any fowls straying on land tenanted by Mr –– will be destroyed.

From an advertisement for Water 4U

HEALTHY CLEAN WATER CAN NOW
BE MADE IN THE CONVENIENCE
OF YOUR OWN HOME

SMALL IS BEAUTIFUL

Small ads. in local newspapers are a perpetual delight and also a rich gold-bearing lode for sociologists.

From the Harrogate Champion Shopper

INVALID chair, 'Dudly Extra plus Electronic' complete with lights, indicators and safety belt, has substantial kerb-crawling facility.

From the Nottingham Evening Post
FOR THE BRIDE
PERSONAL ATTACK ALARM. Feel Safe, the very best in personal protection.

From the Welwyn and Hatfield Times

FIT PERSON wanted to help shoot instructor.

From the Northern Echo

LARGE TRUNK, can be locked, ideal for student or storage, £16.

From the Manchester Evening News

ELSAN TOILET with 1 gall sanitary fluid, used once, slightly damaged.

From the Hampstead and Highgate Express

A BATH late Victorian as used by chartered accountant with clawed feet. Offers?

From the Buckingham Advertiser

Collapsible bed, ideal for guests.

From the Edinburgh Advertiser

DO YOU SCRATCH your bottom in the bath? Have it reglazed by the professional.

From The Guardian

SKI.—SAAS FEE, VERBIER. Mixed parties in chalets bang on slopes, 21st Dec.

From the Edinburgh Advertiser

ANTIQUE piano with candelabra and spiral staircase etc.

From the Sutton Herald

Electric carving knife, brand new, £4. Other baby toys at various prices.

From the Gloucester Citizen

Mop and Bucket Set, contains mop and bucket £3.95.

From the Burnley Citizen

Wanted. Clean babies and small children's clothes, will pay cash.

One morning's ANIMALS AND BIRDS column of The
Times *contained just two items*

BERTIE, extrovert fawn peke puppy, £150.

RELIABLE, adaptable PA overseas sec. exp. 33, domesti-
cated seeks demanding post.

From the Personal Column of the Cyprus Weekly

S. PAROSKOS and Helen Walker would like to announce
that they are no longer engaged.

ENGAGEMENT S. Paroskos of Paphos, Cyprus, and Nicola
Jared of UK would like to announce their engagement.

DANGER! BUREAUCRATS AT WORK

One notable feature of official pronouncements is their almost universal good intentions. Concern for the health, morals and peace of mind of the public is pre-eminent among bureaucratic ideals. Sadly, the English language does not always seem to be able to cope with such high-mindedness.

Instruction issued by the Royal Academy in 1893, concerning regulations to be observed when its female students were permitted to work from a male nude model

It shall be optional for Visitors in the Painting School to set up the male model undraped, except about the loins, to the class of Female Students. The drapery to be worn by the model to consist of ordinary bathing drawers, and a cloth of light material 9 feet long by 3 feet wide, which shall be wound round the loins over the drawers, passed between the legs and tucked in over the waist band; and finally a thin leather strap shall be fastened round the loins in order to insure that the cloth keep its place.

Caution on a Government department form of 1962

Separate departments on the same premises are treated as separate premises for this purpose where separate branches of work which are commonly carried on as separate business in separate premises are carried on in separate departments of the same premises.

Notice in Farringdon Underground Station

Due to staff shortage the automatic ticket machines are not in use.

A London Transport notice of 1973

> Gents and lift out of order
> Please use the stairs

Decree by a French Mayor, 1954

The flights, landings and take-off of airships called 'flying saucers' and 'flying cigars' of any nationality are forbidden on the territory of the community of Châteauneuf-du-Pape.

In the early, heady days of cybertechnology, the compiler of this collection received a computer-generated letter from his local Council, beginning:

Dear Mr Ba, . . .

He subsequently discovered among his neighbours a Mr Obe, a Mr Bart, a Mr Friba, the well-known author Mr Clit and a large number of Mr Esqs. The national press of the time had a field day . . .

If you believe that such problems belong to the past, think again. More recently, the recipient of a wrongly-addressed NSPCC Christmas mail-order catalogue sent in her order and amended the address. The following year two copies of the catalogue arrived, one as before with the right name but the wrong address and the other with the correct address but sent to:

Miss No Surname

Inside, the personalised letter began:

Dear Miss Surname

During the months that followed the computer obviously had second thoughts and decided that 'No' could not possibly be a first name. So, the next Christmas the catalogue duly landed on the doormat addressed to:

Miss N. O. Surname

And thus it has remained.

A letter from Yorkshire Electricity to Mr Arthur Belcher of Huddersfield, who had died the previous year, began:

Dear Mr Deceased . . .

Annotation on a letter returned to the Post Office

Dead. Address unknown.

Local authorities are noted for the comprehensiveness of their mailing lists. Severn and Trent water authority are known to have sent a letter to:

Occupier, Public Convenience . . .

The same organisation, according to the local vicar, addressed a communication to:

The Occupier, Cemetery, Church Road, Burton Joyce.

The Post Office Users National Council once announced:

A request to the Minister for additional staff resources even on a temporary basis, to allow us to achieve a more in-depth customer input into the formulation of Post Office policies, received a sympathetic hearing but a negative response.

Or, 'He wouldn't let us have any more staff.'

Extract from a Department of the Environment short circular detailing the effects of Budget proposals on local authorities

It is clear that a reduction in current expenditure must mean a reduction in jobs.

The circular was signed by seven Under-Secretaries and one Assistant Under-Secretary.

Helpful note from the South Eastern Electricity Board, in their circular If Hardship Hits You, *concerning price increases*

If . . . there is real hardship you can have a slot meter,

but . . . of course, a slot meter will cost you more each quarter.

Amendment to the Hammersmith and Fulham District Plan approved by the Council's Planning Committee
Delete bottlenecks. Insert localised capacity deficiencies.

From the index of the current standing orders of the House of Commons, a few years ago
Scottish Grand Committee
Scottish Standing Committee
Seats: see under Members

Clause in a Connecticut teachers' union contract
Teacher shall make two (2) comments per student per subject, per marking period. One (1) of those comments may be 'no comment', if a second comment concerning the student is inappropriate.

Two managerial edicts that won awards in a contest run by an American magazine
As of tomorrow, employees will only be able to access the building using individual security cards. Pictures will be taken next Wednesday and employees will receive their cards in two weeks.

E-mail is not to be used to pass on information and data. It should be used only for company business.

Ever thoughtful, British Gas provide with their bills a number of helpful notes. Among them is:

To work out the amount of gas you have been charged for, we:

- Take the previous meter reading from the present reading.
- Multiply the answer by 2.83 to give the number of cubic metres of gas supplied. (This step is not needed if you have a new metric meter.)
- Multiply the answer by the Volume Conversion Factor and then by the calorific value shown on the front of this bill.
- Divide the answer by 3.6 to give the number of kilowatt hours (kWh).
- This number is multiplied by the price per kilowatt hour to give the gas charge.

Simple, isn't it?

From a British Railways, Midland Region, bulletin for the use of travel agents' staff

Due to the present paper shortage, with effect from 23rd January, 1974, items appearing on green paper (Special Facilities), will for the time being be printed on red paper. All concerned please note.

From a report in the East Grinstead Advertiser

At the new police headquarters and courthouse at East Grinstead the toilets are marked Ladies and Gentlemen for the magistrates, Men and Women for the public, and Male and Female for the staff.

Notice in the offices of a South London crematorium, listing Important Telephone Numbers. *First on the list is:*

Serious Burns Unit.

A Barclays International announcement in the Daily Nation, Kenya

Barclays Bank Bima House will be closed on Friday 11th June due to the official opening of the premises.

From a story in The Guardian

The Home Office handbook for security officers on how to cope with bombs [gives] in Appendix E '. . . actions to be taken on receipt of a bomb threat'. The list of questions to ask if a terrorist rings you is exhaustive . . . Number eight is: 'What is your name?' and number nine: 'What is your address?'

From a report in The Independent

Novelty condoms will not protect against an unwanted pregnancy, the consumer magazine *Which?* warned yesterday.

However trading standards officers had no objection to novelty condoms—some of which glow in the dark

No person shall walk, run, stand, sit or lie on the grass . . .

or play the Beatles' 'Love Me Do'—provided they were labelled as not being intended for sex.

Extract from VAT News

Notes. Delete the whole of Note (4) and the operative date and substitute the following:-

(4)   Item 1 of the items overriding the exceptions relates to Item 1 of the excepted items; Items 2 and 3 of the items overriding the exceptions relate to Item 2 of the excepted items and Items 4 to 6 of the items overriding the exceptions relate to Item 4 of the excepted items.

Notice-board in Newquay, Cornwall

No person shall walk, run, stand, sit or lie on the grass in this Pleasure Ground.

From a Home Office Standing Conference on Crime Prevention Report

The increase in sexual offences was partly attributable to reported homosexual offences following specific police activity in a public lavatory in Slough.

From a County Council report

. . . For some weeks the method has been tried out at the Guildhall by members of the County Council staff. It is now considered foolproof.

From the Buckinghamshire Leader News and
Advertising

Council chairman Betty Barrett added: 'For 22 years we
have been looking for public toilets.'

Message from the Keeper of Wykehamist Records

It would be a great help if Wykehamists kept the Keeper
informed of interesting appointments, or deaths of themselves or their friends.

*Letter from a local Head of Planning of British
Telecommunications concluded with the immortal words:*

Please let me know if you do not receive this letter.

FOOT IN MOUTH DISEASE

Spokespersons are not the luckiest of public informants. They do not even have the opportunity of reading their sage pronouncements before they are broadcast to the startled world.

From a report in The Independent

A spokesperson for South West Trains said last night: 'Some services have been cut in a bid to reduce over-crowding on trains in the London area.'

From the Swindon Evening Advertiser

Passengers checking the British Rail timetable at Reading Station were shocked to find that the 8.52 a.m. service (to Slough) terminated in Outer Mongolia. A BR spokesman said: 'Our typists put in a word of their choice to remind them to check information. But obviously they forgot to go back.'

A Railtrack spokesman interviewed on BBC Radio News about the Watford train crash:

They should obviously not have been on the same track, although either train could quite legitimately have been there on its own.

From the Daily Telegraph

A member of the platform staff admitted that the station was a bit grubby. 'In the past we've always waited for a strong wind to blow the dust away.'

News item in the Cork Examiner

A spokesman for the ITGWU said in Dublin last night that the British Rail strike, due to begin today, will terminate all services except for passengers on foot.

From the Evening Standard

The night supervisor at the tube station where a body remained undiscovered for eight days has been sacked. [He] was dismissed 24 hours after the man's body was discovered in the women's lavatory at Leytonstone Station.

However, an Underground spokesman today denied that the sacking was linked to the delay in finding the body. Mr B — — had been dismissed 'because he failed to record lost property properly,' he said.

News report in The Guardian

A spokesman for the Water Authorities Association claimed yesterday that there would be no charge for free water after the sell-off.

A letter in The Independent

Sir.—To discover why first-class mail was taking three days to reach us from central London, we rang up Hertford Post Office. 'Oh,' was the reply, 'everything is being delayed because we are having a sales promotion campaign.'

From the Cambrian News

Delighted that his letters started arriving three hours earlier than usual, a former manager of Barmouth asked why. Royal Mail explained that the regular postmen were off sick.

From the Daily Telegraph in 1985

Sarah Ali, one of the nation's most regular savers, has tucked away £2 a week since 1975. It is now worth £1,000. He writes his name on the notes and deposits them in post boxes. Says Sheffield's head postmaster: 'He is someone with a profound misunderstanding of Post Office savings systems.'

From the Stroud News and Journal

Mr John Hole, of Bexbury, Minchinhampton, reported a fault on his line back on 23rd December.

In response to Mr Hole's complaint that no one from BT had let him know what was happening, BT said engineers had tried to contact him several times by telephone.

From The Guardian

A police source said that the incident was being treated as attempted murder and described it as 'a domestic, eternal-triangle-style situation' involving four people.

News item in the East Anglian Daily News

A microwave oven has been stolen from Weeley Crematorium, Clacton police said yesterday.

From the Daily Telegraph

Sgt. Mick Potter of Littlehampton police said, 'Moore obviously aroused the licensee's suspicions as he was the only one in the pub wearing prison uniform.'

Also from the Daily Telegraph

A sex attacker tried to strangle a young woman, cut her throat and then set fire to the bed on which she was lying, police disclosed yesterday.

Dep. Supt. John Jones, leading the search for the woman's attacker, said that he had no doubt that the man was trying to kill her.

Story in The Scotsman

. . . Meanwhile one policeman manning a diversion sign was not slow to grasp the importance of the situation. He said: 'A hole has appeared in the road. Fife police are looking into it.'

From the Financial Times

Former defence minister Alan Clark will not be prosecuted over his evidence in the Matrix Churchill case. The Crown Prosecution Service said police had been 'unable to establish with sufficient certainty which of the inconsistent statements was not true'.

. . . he was the only one in the pub wearing prison uniform.

*Spokesman for BBC Television, following criticism of the
fly-on-the-wall documentary* The Driving School

Some of it was faked. It was a light-hearted documentary.
But the integrity was there.

From a report in the Daily Star

The Advertising Standards Authority said that nudity was
not acceptable in an ad. for Cornish pasties.

From the Hull Daily Mail

A Humberside Police spokesman said: 'We have been
expecting this since it was announced last year.'

BILL OF FARE

These crumbs from restaurant menus constitute a rapid gastronomic tour of the world. Enjoy your meal . . .

A Polish hotel
Salad a firm's own make; limpid red beet soup with cheesy dumplings in the form of fingers; roast duck let loose; beef rashers beaten in the country people's fashion.

A Swiss restaurant
Our wines leave you nothing to hope for.

An Istanbul restaurant
Mixed girrl and baked beings.

A restaurant in Baghdad
Pimps No 1 or Pimps No 2
Shrimps catstails
Escalope Gordon Blue
Cram chaps
Chateaubriani for 3 parsons

A coffee shop in the Rincombe Hotel, Chiang Mai, Thailand

Today's Special: Fried crispy wanton with beef and vegetables.

From a menu in a café near Basingstoke bus station

Egg and Chips; Two Eggs and Chips; Egg, Bacon and Chips; Two Eggs, Bacon and Chips; Sausage and Chips; Two Sausages and Chips; Bacon, Sausage and Chips; Egg, Sausage and Chips; Egg, Two Sausages and Chips; Two Eggs, Sausage and Chips; Two Eggs, Two Sausages and Chips; Egg, Bacon, Sausage and Chips; Two Eggs, Bacon, Two Sausages and Chips; Egg, Bacon, Sausage, Beefburger and Chips . . .

From a menu in Lambeth Social Club

Coffee	35p
Selection of Sandwiches	from 60p
Cheese or Pate Ploughpersons	from £1.50

BED AND BOARD

One expects hotels abroad to wrestle with the English language, but British establishments seem to have the same problem . . .

A clutch of notices in hotels: this one in a Belgrade hotel lift

To move the cabin, push button for wishing floor. If the cabin should enter more persons, each one should press number of wishing floor. Driving is then going alphabetically by natural order.

In Southport

BATHS may be had (by arrangement) with the manageress only.

Somewhere in England

If requiring breakfast please hang on door knob before 7 a.m.

In Moscow, across the road from a Russian Orthodox monastery

You are welcome to visit the cemetery where famous Russian and Soviet composers, artists, and writers are buried daily except Thursday.

Beside a telephone in a hotel on the shores of Lake Titicaca, South America

Mr Passing. If it did not obtain you response until the third stamped, I will serve you to cut the call and return to attempt it, thus avoided you the unnecessary connection of their it's your his called since telephony system register the call as of the stamped quarter though may not have been obtained response.

In a Helsinki hotel bedroom

In the hotel restaurant the waitress will give you a bill and you may sign her on the back side.

In Paris

Please leave your valise at the front people.

In a small hotel in the Dordogne

In the event of fire, the visitor, avoiding haste, is to walk down the corridor and warm the chambermaid.

In Japanese hotels

Sports jackets may be worn but no trousers
No smoking in bed nor other disgusting behaviour

Advertisement for a Bavarian hotel

Well led hotel with comfort of nowadays and hot and cold water running through all the bedrooms.

. . . and hot and cold water running through all the bedrooms.

Sign in a window in a Scottish village
Bed & Breakfast with Local Honey

Placard in the Thousand Islands district in Canada
Restaurant
Live Lobsters
Dancing Nightly

Advertisement in Blackmore Vale Magazine
BLACK DOG INN, Chilmark, Now Serving Sunday Lunch-
eon in the new Restaurant. Telephone for reservations.
If you eat here you won't get better.

Sign in a shop window in Eastbourne
All sausages made with the best conservatives.

Instruction on a room voucher for the Hotel Columbus, Bremen
Breakfast ist obligatory!

Fire instructions in a Richmond public house
In case of fire stand on head and bang knob on
ground.

Sign in a café in a French village
Persons are requested not to occupy seats in this café
without consummation.

Advertisement in the Bedford Herald

Surma Tandoori
Restaurant
Where East meets West
Dine in style and enjoy superb Indian and Tandoori
cuisine in Bedford's Premier Indian Restaurant
Full licensed   Full take-away service
Authentic Indian Doctor

Poster seen in a Home Counties town

Come to the new ––– Tandoori. One visit and you will
always be regular.

Advertisement in the Caterer and Hotel Keeper

SINGLE HANDED CHEF
for
Small Luxury Hotel
Dartmoor National Park
Maximum thirty discriminating guests.

This will suit a young fully qualified chef who wants to
earn a reputation or an older qualified chef who wants
a less demanding position.

Advertisement in Niugini Nius, *Papua, New Guinea*

Wednesday, Thursday and Friday
Evenings
Uwe Fock entertains on the
Organ in the Dining Room

EN ROUTE

The particular challenge for the author of road signs is their necessary brevity. Travel literature, on the other hand, whatever the mode of transport, imposes no such restriction but common sense still seems to be elusive . . .

Are koala bears notoriously bad-tempered? A road sign on the Pacific Highway near Sydney, Australia
DANGER! KOALAS CROSS AT NIGHT

English street signs
P at any time.

Buses only. Except buses.

English road signs
No overtaking for the next 200 yrs.

Site entrance. Please enter from opposite direction.

Drive slowly and allow cows to pass.

Hallwood Hospital. Strictly no admittance.

Road sign near Liskeard, Cornwall
DANGER! Low Flying Owls.

Sign outside Marlow, Buckinghamshire
Little Marlow Cemetery—no through road.

Sign on the M40 Motorway
Emergency WC 20 miles.

From a letter in the Daily Telegraph
In the past few days, the royal blue sign on entering Berkshire from Wiltshire, which read 'Royal County of Berkshire', has been replaced by a green and grey sign reading 'Welcome to West Berkshire, Home of the Newbury Building Society'.

Kenyan road sign
No entry. In only.

Ugandan road sign
Special force training area. Restricted to unauthorised persons.

A translated instruction said to have been handed to English-speaking competitors in a motoring event in Mexico City
Competitors will defile themselves on the promenade at 11 a.m., and each car will have two drivers who will relieve themselves at each other's conveniences.

*Advice given by a Turkish newspaper to drivers whose cars
have plunged into the Bosphorus*

If the vehicle continues to descend, put on the handbrake.

From an early car instruction manual

In practice it will be found that sufficient force on the
handbrake to hold the car will force the brake pedal backwards until the driver's foot may be removed altogether.

Warning from a 1901 Lanchester Driving Manual

A skilled driver will never, under any circumstances,
collide with a kerb broadside on. If necessary, he will
exaggerate a side-slip sufficiently to negotiate the kerb
backwards.

*The above stricture may account for a helpful note in a 1912
catalogue from the same manufacturer*

Steering system—optional.

*Notice displayed on the counter of the Dutch Railways travel
bureau in Amsterdam*

No train information. No boat information. No international tickets. No maps of the city. Tourist and Hotel
Information—not here.

From Oman Airways in-flight magazine

Our Barman Recommends Cocktail of the Week:
'MID AIR COLLISION'

Cocktail of the Week . .

From the magazine of the Motor Caravanners' Club

Regretfully, a favourite village hall used by Surrey members especially for barn dancing, the large one at Bletchingley, will not be available to us this autumn. Sudden wall-cracks have appeared after our community singing last December and the future of the hall is in doubt.

From a promotional booklet issued by a New York travel agency

British Railways are used by all classes of the community. If you stand and watch commuters arriving at any of the London termini you will see for yourself that they are a cross section of the community.

Legend on a Spanish airline's sick bag

BAG TO BE USED IN
CASE OF SICKNESS OR
TO GATHER REMAINS

Brass notice plate on SS Earl Sigurd, *the last steamship to serve the Orkney Islands*

The deck from the bulkhead at aft end of the bridge to 6.6 ft aft of this deckhouse contains 326 sq ft & is certified for 36 first class passengers when not occupied by animals, cargo or other encumbrance.

Sign at a Texas airport

Jet blast is dangerous. Passengers only beyond this point.

Advertisement in the Daily Mail

CABIN STAFF

Laker Airways require Cabin Staff for their Gatwick Base. All applicants must be between 20 and 33 years old. Height 5' 4" to 5' 10". Education to GCE standard. Must be able to swim.

PRINTERS' PIE

Misprints, like the poor, are always with us. From time to time, however, the wandering fingers of the typesetter can be charmingly creative.

Small ad. in the Lost and Found column of a South African newspaper
One white Rabbi, with brown ears. Found hopping down 3rd Avenue.

Advertisement in the Andover Advertiser
Bungalow: 3 bedrooms, lounge, dining-room diner/kitchen, bathroom, coloured suite, toilet 2 miles Andover.

From the Belfast Telegraph *Pet's Corner*
Wanted: Male standard Datsun puppy.

From the Nottingham Evening Post
Attractive woman, 32, new to area, looking for attractive man between 30–435 for friendship.

From the Hitchin, Letchworth and Baldock Herald

Naturist male, 38, seeks lady to accompany him on trips. She should be uninhabited and adventurous.

From a list of Starters on a menu at Brynmeadows Golf Club, South Wales

Petite Choux Buns Filled With Chicken Liver Forcemeat placed on a pool of recurrent sauce.

A Sadlers Wells programme explained that the ballet 'The Green Table':

. . . takes its title from a green baize table, flanked by powerful business men and rich magnets.

Advertisement in a Wroxham supermarket

Pro Shiatsh all over body portable massager relives aches and pains.

And one in the Wimbledon Guardian

BRAND NEW three pink bridesmaids, dresses plus accessories £35 each.

Notice in the Leamington Spa Observer

The Observer wishes to apologise for a typesetting error in our Tots and Toddlers advertising feature last week which led to Binswood Nursery School being described as serving 'children casserole' instead of chicken casserole.

From What's On, When and Where, *East Anglia*
23 August 11 September
9.00 am Daily except Saturdays. Finals held on Friday of
each week.
GREAT YARMOUTH OPEN BOWELS FESTIVAL

Advertisement in The County Times & Express &
Gazette, *Newtown*
HAROLD PINTER'S THE CAKETAKER

Small ad. in the Wandsworth Times
TELEPHONE EXTENSION socket kit, 30 metres £8. Small
electric organ, good for learning £300 ono. Also large
Orgasm.

*From the title page of the second issue of an air travel
publication*
AIR CHINA INFRIGHT MAGAZINE

From the Banbury Guardian
Hand made painted Nativity set complete with Manager.

*Notice from the Wilmslow & District Orchestral Society,
Cheshire*
Dear Patron or Non-playing Member,
The orchestra will be holding its annual cheese and wind
party on Friday, June 16th at 8.00 p.m.

Advertised in The Times, Daily Telegraph *and*
Independent

A Valentine's Night Concert
and your chance to view
hearts, flowers and genital jewellery
at
Royal Festival Hall

*The Band of the Royal Air Force Regiment in Keighley,
West Yorkshire, announced in its programme*
Elgar's 'Pomp and Circulation March No 1'.

Notice in Boots, Banbury
A saving of £5 on items bought singularly.

From the Northampton Chronicle & Echo
Antique stuffed peasant in presentation box.

Sign in the Key Health Club, Nottingham
Ladies Changing Rooms. Please bare with us during
improvements.

From an advertisement in Free Newspaper, *West Sussex*
CAR BOOB SALE

PROCEED WITH CARE

During November 1997, *The Times* letters page published an enthusiastic exchange of correspondence on the subject of helpful information offered by manufacturers and other traders—who appear to have a low opinion of the intelligence of their customers or, perhaps, a justified fear of their customers' lawyers. Here are the highlights.

From a 'flower and plant guide' supplied with a flower arrangement

Candles. These are for decoration only. To avoid the risk of fire you are advised not to light them. *(Mrs Victoria Barnett, Monkseaton)*

Instructions on a packaged bread and butter pudding

Important. Take Care. Product will be hot after heating. *(Mrs Sylvia Ray, Exford)*

Caption to a picture of a solitary clove of garlic on a supermarket tub of garlic

Serving suggestion. *(Mr Chris Ancliff, London)*

Instruction accompanying a new hot-water bottle

When filling the bottle do not use boiling water or water from the hot tap as this will cause the bottle to perish. *(Mrs Lucy Amos, Bath)*

Instructions for a compact camera

Do not use this camera when it is emitting smoke or is unusually hot to the touch . . . Use of the camera in any of these conditions may cause a fire . . . *(Mr Phil Gulliford, Purley-on-Thames)*

Warning on a pack of sleeping tablets

May cause drowsiness. *(Mr Peter Orr, Guisborough)*

Instruction on a tube of hand-cream

Apply sparingly before and after you use your hands. *(Mrs Margot Turnbull, Bevere)*

Warning on a small knife with a retractable blade

Keep out of children. *(Mrs Joan New, Harnham)*

Instruction on a packet of peperoni

Do not eat packaging. *(Mr Colin Mackay, Mount Laurel, NJ)*

Inscription on the rear bumpers of a fleet of mammoth 16-wheel trucks

Do not push. *(Mr Michael Vaisey, Little Gransden)*

Warning on a pack of Valium prescribed by a vet for a nervous springer spaniel

May cause drowsiness. If affected do not drive. *(Mr Anthony Abrahams, Cowley)*

Instruction on an NHS General Ophthalmic Services prescription supplied by an optician to a patient suffering from long-sightedness

Read the rest of this form before you get your spectacles. *(Dr Antony Warren, Cambridge)*

Advice to the purchaser of a pair of binoculars

Remove the dust from the lenses with a camel's hairbrush. *(Mr F. E. Hobbs, Compton)*

To conform with the relevant British Standard, a manufacturer of glass-door cabinets is required to affix the following label to his products:

Do not hit the glass with hard or sharp objects. *(Mr Roger Richardson, Beaver & Tapley Ltd, Southall)*

Instructions on a hand-drier in the gents' lavatory of a five-star hotel in Botswana

Shake water off hands
Rub gently under blower
Wipe on shirt
(Mr R. K. Day, Comberbach)

It is not only readers of *The Times* who have encountered such helpful advice. Here are some other gleanings.

Notice on the lid of a jar of hot pickles
Press and then push off.

Label on the product of a well-known store
These wrought-iron candlesticks will age with time. Rusting is an intrinsic quality of the metal.

Instruction accompanying a paint-stripper capable of delivering a blast of hot air at 500°C
Never use as a hair drier.

Warning on a potted basil plant
Only eat the leaves and stem of this plant. Do not eat the roots or soil.

Helpful hint on a leaflet from a retailer selling curtains
ORDER TWO if pair required.

HOLY, HOLY, HOLY

One might imagine that Divine guidance would render this section unnecessary. Fortunately, it not only exists but its items can only be described as inspired.

Message from the Rector of Cliffe and Cooling, Kent, in the parish newsletter
I am always particularly glad to hear of any cases of sickness, especially when they are long term.

Church notice from St John's, Danbury
The Rev. Andrew Adano, a nomad priest from North Kenya, will be coming to Danbury next Sunday for a week's stay at the Rectory. Anyone wishing to have him for a meal during his stay should ask the Rector, please.

Newsletter of the parishes of Bessingby and Carnaby, Yorkshire

April	23	Wednesday	St George, Patron Saint of England
	25	Friday	St Mark Evangelist
	27	Sunday	Easter 3
May	1	Thursday	SS Philip & James, Apostles & Martyrs
	3	Saturday	Rugby League Cup Final

Notice outside a spiritualist church in Worthing
No healing in August.

Sign outside an Italian hospital run by nuns
These little sisters solicit alms, they do not respect religion and harbour all manner of disease.

And another, outside a Berkshire school
St Margaret's School of the Immaculate Conception for Girls
Preparatory for Boys

Wayside Sermon poster outside an English church
Don't let worry kill you off. Let the Church help.

Sign at a Rangoon temple
Foot wearing prohibited. Socks not allowed.

From a report in The Guardian
A run of posters have appeared in a post office by the river Tamar. The first advertised that the Vicar would give a talk entitled 'Jesus Walks on Water'. The following week's lecture was billed as 'The Search for Jesus'.

Announcement in the West Chiddington Parish Magazine
Tonight the sermon topic will be 'What is Hell?' Come early and listen to the choir.

Notice placed by the Harewood Christian Discussion Group in Collingham Parish Magazine

We shall be meeting on Wednesday 11th April when the subject will be 'Heaven. How do we get there?' Transport is available at 7.55 p.m. from the bus stop opposite the Harewood Arms.

From the parish magazine of the Church of St Edmund and St Mary, Ingatestone

A special welcome to the Alexander family as they give thanks for the birth of their child during the morning service.

Sign in a rural churchyard

Anyone having relatives buried in this churchyard is asked to be so good as to keep them in order.

Announcement in the YWCA centenary magazine, Sydney

Discussion groups are being held on the Third World War—beginning 14th July.

Message from a vicar in a parish magazine

The headmaster will preach at the Parish Church on Sunday, May 13th, and another of the staff on May 6th. On both these Sundays I hope to be away on holiday.

'Heaven. How do we get there?' Transport is available . . .

EXCUSE MY FRENCH

Strictly speaking, the following extracts from foreign language phrase-books and dictionaries are not public notices at all. Yet they do provide instructions, more or less reliable, when their owners are literally at a loss for words. Imagine the plight of the nineteenth-century traveller without the help given by his phrase-book, enabling him to utter the celebrated cry of 'Help! Help! The postillion has been struck by lightning!'

From an English-Albanian phrase-book
Tell the Italian consul to fetch me an omelette.

From an old Finnish phrase-book
Excuse me, I hate to trouble you, but your motor-cycle is standing on my foot.

And from a French-English one
'Why do you not dance with Hélène?'
'I cannot, because she is smoking and I am wearing a celluloid collar.'

Phrases found by Time Magazine *in a Russian-English language guide published in the, then, Soviet Union*

Flying in the TU-114 I felt myself excellently.
Please give me curds, sower cream, fried chicks, pulled bread and one jelly-fish.
I want my hair frizzled.
Show us your devices for outer space research work.
How powerful is this reactor? Shew me a working diagram of this reactor.
Whose invention is this? When was this invention patented? This is a Soviet invention.

Two useful phrases from a Chinese-English dictionary

I am sorry that your concubine is sick.
Here comes the Executioner.

SPECIAL OFFERS

Special Offers exhibit an enthusiasm which seems to dazzle advertisers, let alone potential customers.

A tear-off slip at the bottom of a leaflet from a Hampshire boat-builder

Please send me . . . yachts at the 1980 Autumn price of £28,000 + VAT.

Notice outside a Do-It-Yourself store in Wiltshire

Special offer: Disappearing loft ladders. Only two left.

Advertisement in a nudists' magazine

Naturist's Motor Cycle for sale. Fur saddle and vacuum flask holder. Solar heated crash helmet. Will exchange for clothes.

From a New York bookseller's catalogue

This is one of the rarest works on cannibalism (with 10 plates cloth).

Situation vacant advertisement for Funeral Operatives in Colchester

Good rates of pay and staff discount.

Good rates of pay and staff discount.

Offer in a toy-seller's catalogue
Pregnant doll—extraordinary Danish conception.

Advertisement by the Redbridge Sports Centre
This offer only applies to new members or members who
have expired over a year ago.

Item on a price list Clothes for Your Honeymoon *issued
by a West Midlands store*
Silk and lace nightdress (in case).

Photographer's advertisement in the Neath Guardian
We shoot Children
on Wednesdays
Without Appointments

MEDICAL MATTERS

The remarkable dedication of our National Health staff is demonstrated below in their regular attendance at lectures, conferences and seminars.

From an advertisement in The Times

THE MIDDLESEX HOSPITAL
Mortimer Street, London, W.1
WANTED
SPARE RIGHT HAND

Medical announcement

Royal College of Physicians of Edinburgh
Annual Collegiate Members' Symposium
WHAT TO DO IN THE MIDDLE OF THE NIGHT:
(Organ Failure—The First Few Hours)

From a Leeds University diary of events

Physiology Seminar—the value of a vagally innervated gastric antrum and intact pylorus in the surgery of peptic ulcer. Buffet afterwards.

From St Mary's Hospital Medical Staff Newsletter

June 9th   Mr GLEN TILLOTSON (Bayer)
Traveller's diarrhoea
Sandwiches provided

Excerpt from a programme of a Royal College of Physicians conference

9.50:   Alcohol and the heart.
10.20: Alcohol and the nervous system.
11.20: Effects of alcohol on the gastrointestinal
        system.
12.10: Nutrition and alcohol.
12.40: Bar open.

Hints given to prospective contributors to the British Medical Journal

Obituaries must be submitted exclusively to the BMJ and should be under 250 words; we give preference to those submitted within three months of the person's death. We welcome self-written obituaries and good quality recent photographs, and, as a medical journal, we encourage authors to include the cause of death.

Advertisement in the Leicester Mercury

INFIRMARY OPERATIC
SOCIETY
MALE MEMBERS
URGENTLY REQUIRED

From a report noted in the Bury Times

Accident and emergency cases assessed within five months of arrival: 100%.

SITS VACANT

A recurring delight to be found in newspapers' Situations Vacant columns is employers' wayward use of the English language, a defect they would deplore in their applicants.

Seen in the Okehampton Times
Steward/stewardess to the British Legion Club. Experience essential but not necessary.

From an advertisement for staff at Ramsay Golf Club, Isle of Man
The Steward will be responsible for running the bar. The Stewardess will be responsible for catering and taking the profits.

From the New Civil Engineer *magazine for senior structural engineers*
The North Sea is our business—why not drop in?

Instruction on a local Council job application form for school leavers
Give the names and addresses of two referees. They should not be your schoolteachers but responsible persons of mature age who are well acquainted with you.

From the British Bandsman

Accountant for newly established medicentre polyclinic, Riyadh, Saudi Arabia. Trombone player preferred.

From The Stage

Wanted: 8 authentic Japanese Equity members to work on BBC2 serial 'Heart of the Country'. One problem. All these Japanese ladies and gentlemen should be over 35, and live in the area of Shepton Mallet.

From the Milton Keynes Gazette

Part-time Job
An unexpected vacancy for a
KNIFE THROWER'S ASSISTANT

Advertisement in the Hendon Times

Swimming Teachers required for both Children & Adults, ASA Qualified. Must be prepared to go in the water.

From the Leicester Mercury

Young carpet salesman required, 5-day week, good salary and conditions. Basic plus commission. Free use of the company's toilet.

From the Sheffield Star

Rotherham Metropolitan Borough Council. Temporary crematorium assistant required (The Council operates a non-smoking policy).

An unexpected vacancy . . .

Two advertisements from the UK Press Gazette

Bella. Britain's latest magazine for women is looking for fast, accurate **sub-editors** who can turn out bright copy and captions without forgetting to cross the i's and dot the t's.

Editorial staff and freelance writers required for *Sewer and Sewerage*, a new trade paper for the effluent disposal industry. Applicants should have a keen interest in the subject and related products.

From the Southern Star, *Skibbereen*

YOUTH WANTED—To train as Petrol Pump Attendant. 5-day week, Mon to Sat p.m. Elderly man would suit.

Advertisement by an operatic society in the Luton Post

WANTED

ACTORS—SINGERS—DANCERS

MEN PARTICULARLY

STAGE STAFF. Sex immaterial but
an advantage

From the Cheltenham and District Shopping News

Full-time and Part-time
Women/Girls Required

CRUMPET DEPARTMENT

HOMES, SWEET HOMES

The Properties Misdescriptions Act initially curbed the creative talents of estate agents. Now they have to play safe and resort to those old standbys, the meaningless adjective and the lyrical but unspecific. Nonetheless, they still manage to whip themselves into a froth of excitement. Currently, on a word-count of a set of Sunday papers, the most-used description is 'stunning'.

From The Sunday Times

This mews house has real personality! It welcomes you with a 'hello' and says 'please come and live here'. **N.B. For the purposes of the Properties Misdescriptions Act please note that this is not really a talking house!**

Another advertisement in the same issue of The Sunday Times *may mean more than the copywriter intended*

... Where the gentle waters of the Thames wake you in the morning ...

In a list of properties to be sold, a West London auctioneer included a block of flats in Muswell Hill, offering vacant possession. A footnote added:

TO VIEW: By courtesy of the squatters.

A town house in Bayswater was offered with:
Full vacant position.

From some years ago, a choice property proposition:
On Sussex coast urgent sale required, lucrative Old People's Home. Self-contained accommodation 14 persons. Fully equipped, no qualified staff.

Advertisement in the Evening Standard
N.W.1. Large sunny room + amenities, middle-aged man available soon.

Advertisement in The Observer
Architect's Own House: Elegantly restored Victorian terrace house in original Georgian style. Must be viewed. Offers over £297,000.

House agents' sign
Joint Sole Agents

'House for rent' advertisement in The Times
BRONTE COUNTRY—17th-century luxury cottage. Ideal honeymoon. Sleeps 2/5,

Another house to rent, offered in The Times
A Manor house with 5 recs, 10 beds, 4 baths, 5 acres, lake, stables, dovecote, dead gardener. 80 mins Waterloo. £600 pw.

BRONTE COUNTRY . . . luxury cottage . . .

SINGULAR GEMS

Variety is the spice of announcements to the public. Here is a selection of splendidly idiosyncratic items.

Announcement in the Eastern Evening News

DRAINAGE DEMONSTRATION CANCELLED
Unfortunately the drainage demonstration which was to be held at Woodton on May 19th has had to be cancelled due to wet site conditions.

From a list of Honorary Life Members of the Maidenhead Amateur Operatic Society

The late Mrs A. Whitford.

From Universal Yacht Signals, *by George Holland Ackers, 1890s*

Hoist 5761: Can I have . . . quarts of turtle soup?
Hoist 9852: Marmalade—orange unless specified.
Hoist 6419: I can strongly recommend my washerwoman

From a letter to parents from a Somerset school

The Parents' Association has arranged for a representative of the Association on Alcoholism to speak to the school. He is an excellent speaker and will probably be willing to have a 'quick one' with some of us after the evening is over.

Notice at doors of Woolworth's store in Eastbourne
No smoking, guide dogs excepted.

Spotted in the USA
For those of you who have small children and don't know it we have a nursery downstairs.

Sign at a location so far unidentified
Up steps to sunken garden.

From an Exeter Rugby Club match programme
Captain's Disco. Notice to all players, this is a compulsory event and takes place on Saturday 22nd December. Those not attending will face stiff penalties. Females are being arranged and there will be a very pleasant happy hour.

From the programme of a horticultural show
Baby Show: best baby under six months; best baby under twelve months; best baby under two years . . .
Rules for Exhibitors: all exhibits become the property of the Committee as soon as staged and will be sold for the benefit of the Hospital at the termination of the Exhibition.

From a rose-grower's catalogue
LADY BLENKINSOP: Delightful in a bed, but superb against a wall.

CHESTNUTS

Quietly, unsuspected, a surprising number of examples of the public banana skin have entered folk memory. As yet, no one has traced their origins. Even if such widely-known specimens are not always authentic, they certainly ought to be.

Notice in a hotel in India, Mexico and no doubt elsewhere

All the water in this establishment has been personally passed by the Manager.

Said to have been seen in Yorkshire

DO NOT THROW STONES AT THIS NOTICE.

Advertisement for an Italian hotel

French widows in every bedroom affording delightful prospects.

Sent to members of a London gentlemen's club

You are reminded that you may not bring your mistress into the club unless, of course, she is the wife of another member.

French widows in every bedroom . . .

Small ad. in a local newspaper
FOR SALE: Wedding dress (unused) and pair of spiked running shoes.

Another small ad. of unidentified origin
Mr and Mrs – – have left off clothing of every description, and invite inspection.

Notice in a Battersea Park newsagent's shop
Dog for sale. Eats anything. Fond of children.

Sign on a post in the middle of a ford in a country lane
If you cannot read this notice the water is too deep for motor vehicles.

Small ad. in the Kent and Sussex Courier
32-year-old male wishes to meet lady with own car in return for love and affection, would appreciate photo of car.

From an unidentified leaflet
Can you afford to be let down nowadays? Then deal with Messrs – – – Ltd.

Small ad. in a local newspaper
For sale: Bath for baby with tin bottom.

From an advertisement, supposedly in a New Zealand newspaper

Why rend your garments elsewhere when our up to date laundry can do the job more effectively?

Nineteenth-century sign in a lodging house window, later adapted as the title of a music hall song

Gentlemen taken in and done for.

THINGS TO COME

Advertisement on a Website for an aeronautical engineer required to work on Jupiter's moon, Europa

Must be willing to travel.